Contents

Words that appear in **bold** can be found in the glossary on page 30.

The Geography Detective, Sherlock Bones, will help you learn all about Pollution. The answers to Sherlock's questions can be found on page 31.

What is pollution?

The natural world around us is called the **environment**. It is made up of the air, the land and the oceans. When the environment is damaged by harmful substances, we call it **pollution**. Pollution can affect the air, water or soil as well as the plants, animals and people that rely on them.

Some pollution happens naturally. For example when a volcano erupts, red-hot lava burns the countryside. The biggest eruptions release a huge cloud of ash that can spread around the world. The cloud partly blocks sunlight, which can make the climate cooler for a short time. However this only happens occasionally. Most pollution is caused by people and happens regularly.

Erupting volcanoes, such as Mount Pinatubo in the Philippines, pour huge amounts of ash and gas into the atmosphere.

Light and sound

Noise and light pollution can both harm wildlife. In the oceans, whales and dolphins use sound to find their way. Noise from ships' engines can confuse them, so they become lost and get stranded on beaches. Bright lights make it more difficult for owls and bats to hunt at night.

Planes flying low overhead can be incredibly noisy.

There are many different kinds of pollution. Pollution can take the form of gas such as smoke from a factory. It can be liquid, such as an oil spill, or solid, such as litter dropped on the street.

Many types of pollution can be seen, but some types, such as some **radioactive** waste, are invisible. Noise, heat and light are also forms of pollution. The harmful substances that cause pollution are called **pollutants**. These are usually waste products of various kinds, which are just dumped instead of being **disposed** of safely. This book will help you to investigate the causes of pollution. It will also explain what is being done about pollution, and how we can all help to protect our environment.

DETECTIVE WORK

How noisy is your neighbourhood? Stand outside at different times of day. Rate the noise level on a scale of 1 to 10, where 1 is very quiet, and 10 is incredibly noisy. Think about what is causing the noise – is it passing traffic, trains or aircraft, music or machinery?

What are the main causes of pollution?

Sadly, pollution is a fact of modern life. Farming, mining and industry are some of the biggest polluters. But we all add some pollution to the natural world, as we go about our daily lives at home and at school.

Using energy causes a lot of pollution. Every time we switch on a light or computer, we use electricity. This is made in power stations that mostly burn coal, oil or gas. These so-called **fossil fuels** release waste that can cause pollution when they are burned. Electricity is very convenient – so convenient we often waste it, for example when we leave lights shining all night. Factories, farms, shops and offices all use a lot of electricity. Cars, buses, trains and planes also produce pollutants as they burn fuel.

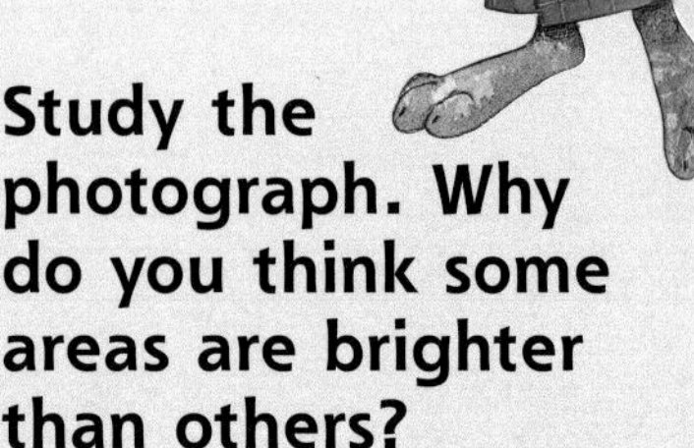

Study the photograph. Why do you think some areas are brighter than others?

This photo, taken from space, shows North America lit up at night.

Shops and supermarkets are full of goods, from processed foods to computers and other machinery. All these things are made from natural produce or **raw materials**. Factories of all kinds can produce pollutants as they process materials. The factories, therefore, cause a lot of pollution. More pollution can be produced as goods are packaged and then transported to shops for us to buy.

Some forms of pollution last only a short time. For example, smoke from a bonfire disappears quickly. Other forms last much longer. Electricity is also made using nuclear fuel. But this produces radioactive waste that remains dangerous for thousands of years.

FOCUS ON

Accidental and routine pollution

Pollution sometimes results from accidents. It also happens routinely, as a result of everyday activities. In 1986, the River Rhine was badly polluted by chemicals following a fire at a riverside factory in Switzerland. The pollution killed river life as far as 100 kilometres downstream. However at the time, the Rhine was also regularly polluted by factories along its banks.

DETECTIVE WORK

In many parts of the world, lights hide the night sky. Carry out a light survey. Look out of a top-floor window on a clear night. Can you see the stars, or are they hidden by local lights? What types of lights can you see – street lamps, car headlights, lighted buildings? If you live in the country, can you see the glow of a distant town?

Factories by the Rhine produce pollution as they use energy and process raw materials. Nowadays, however, there are strict laws about pollution along the river.

How does pollution affect the natural world?

Pollution can spread through the air, water or soil. Winds carry air pollution a long way. Waves, tides and currents spread pollution at sea. Trickling water spreads pollution through the soil. Traces of pollution are found even in remote places, far from farms, factories and towns.

This seal has got tangled up in a fishing net. Seals can also die if they swallow plastic that they mistake for food.

Wildlife can be harmed by solid forms of waste, such as litter. For example, animals can be injured by rusty cans and broken glass. Living things can also be harmed by waste gases or liquids. Trees can be damaged by smoke or fumes which they absorb through their leaves. They can soak up polluted water with their roots.

The living things in an environment depend on one another for food. For this reason, pollution can spread through the natural world via food chains.

Pollution in the Arctic

Very high levels of pollution have been found in Inuit people living in the remote Arctic. Their diet contains a lot of meat from seals and whales. These animals have absorbed pollution from their prey.

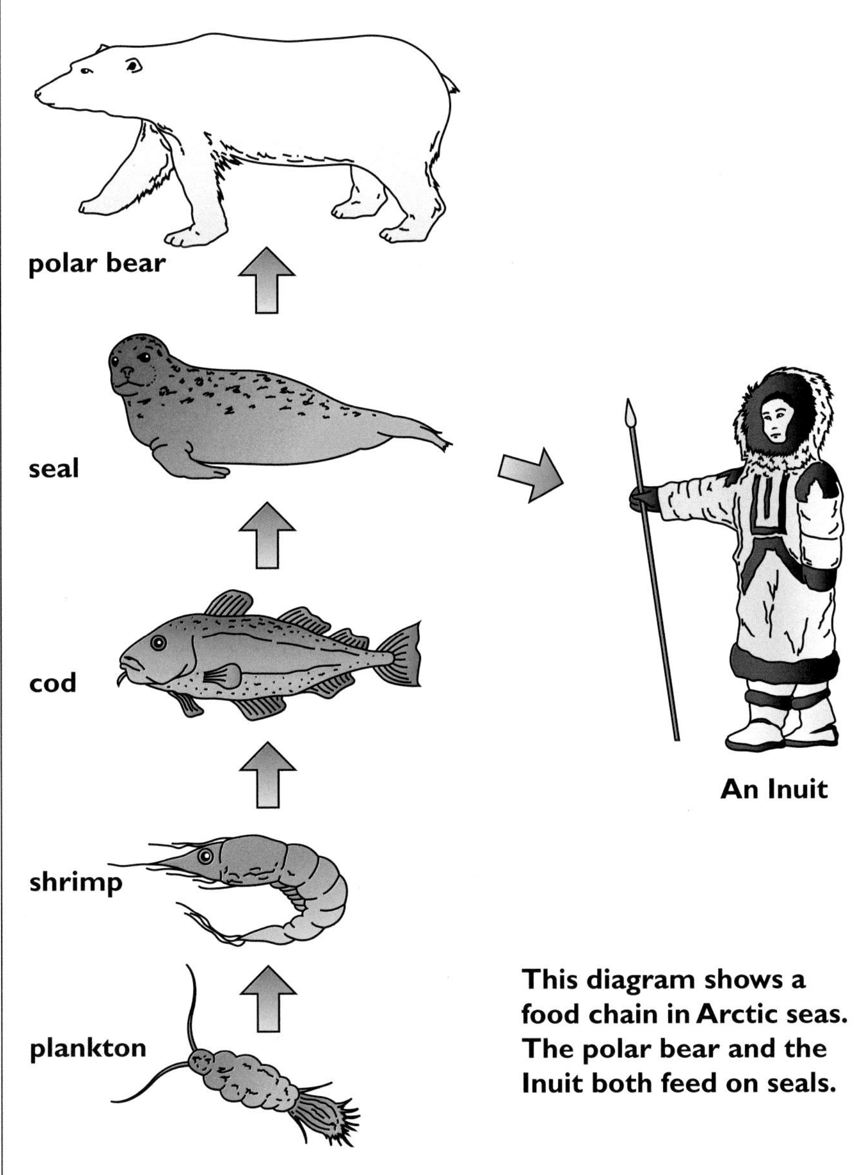

This diagram shows a food chain in Arctic seas. The polar bear and the Inuit both feed on seals.

DETECTIVE WORK

Carry out a litter survey in your neighbourhood. Count the amount of litter you can see on your street, in the school grounds and the local park. What types of litter are causing pollution– is it paper, plastic, food trays, bottles or cans?

In the oceans, tiny plankton form the base of the food chain. If plankton absorb pollution in the water, it passes on to shrimps that eat the plankton. Fish that eat many shrimps get a higher dose of pollution. At the top of the chain, polar bears contain high levels of pollution because they eat many polluted prey.

People as well as animals can be harmed by pollution in the food chain. In the 1950s, the people of Minimata Bay in Japan started to get sick. The problem was traced to mercury poisoning. This dangerous metal was used by local factories and then dumped in the bay. There it was absorbed by fish and shellfish. People who ate seafood got sick too.

Study the food chain. What animals prey on fish? What is the main food of polar bears?

What problems are caused by air pollution?

The air in the **atmosphere** is mostly made up of nitrogen and oxygen, but also contains **water vapour**, carbon dioxide and other gases. Clean air is vital to all living things, including people. However factories, power stations and also vehicles produce a lot of air pollution as they burn fossil fuels.

A dirty haze called **smog** is a problem in many large cities. Smog results when waste gases from industry and vehicles react with sunlight. The poisonous haze can give people breathing problems such as asthma. In some cities, cyclists and some people who work outdoors, such as traffic police, wear masks to avoid breathing in poisonous fumes.

Reducing smog

Devices called **catalytic converters** are now fitted to car exhausts to filter out some harmful waste gases. Lead also used to be added to petrol, but scientists discovered that lead pollution was very harmful. So in most countries, petrol is now lead-free.

A cloud of smog hangs over Beijing, China. The problem is worst in calm or warm, sunny weather.

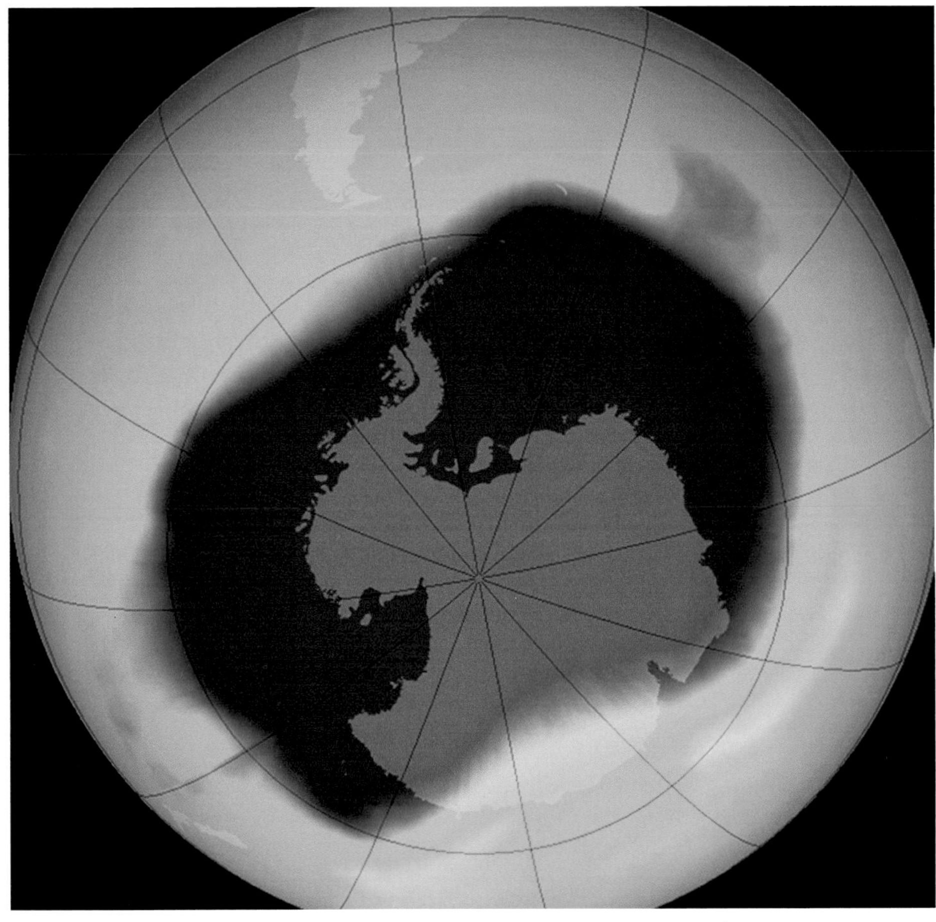

This false-colour image shows ozone loss over Antarctica in 2006. The 'hole' where ozone is thinnest is shown in purple.

DETECTIVE WORK

Check for air pollution in your area. You will need three pot or jar lids smeared with petroleum jelly. Put the lids outdoors in different places – for example, in the garden, on the street and in the park. Check the lids after a day. Which lid has attracted the most dirt?

The **ozone layer** high in the atmosphere helps shield us from harmful rays in sunlight. The harmful rays are called **ultraviolet rays** or UV rays. In the 1980s, scientists discovered that the ozone layer had got much thinner, especially over the polar regions. Something was destroying ozone.

UV rays can cause health problems such as skin cancer. That's why it's important to wear suntan cream when you are outdoors in sunny weather. Eventually scientists realised that chemicals called **CFCs** were harming ozone.

CFCs were used in the **manufacture** of fridges, aerosol cans and foam packaging. Countries around the world agreed to stop using them. Scientists hope the ozone layer will start to recover now we are no longer using CFCs.

What is acid rain?

Acid rain is another problem caused by air pollution. Waste gases from industry and cars cause rain to become slightly acidic. Acid rain is an example of how pollution can pass from the air to affect water supplies and the soil.

These fir trees in the Czech Republic have been killed by acid rain.

About 50 years ago, scientists in Sweden noticed that local forests were being harmed by something. The leaves of trees were brown and shrivelled. Some trees were dying. Scientists traced the problem to certain gases – sulphur dioxide released by factories, and nitrogen oxides from cars. When these waste gases mix with moisture in the air, they produce rain that is acidic.

Forests in industrial parts of Europe and North America were suffering from acid rain damage. But so were forests in remote parts of Sweden. Winds can waft polluted air for hundreds of kilometres.

DETECTIVE WORK

Check for signs of acid rain damage in your area. Damaged trees have bare branches. In towns, look for stone statues and buildings that are worn and are badly eroded. You can find out more about acid rain using the Internet.

Damage from acid rain

Acid rain not only harms living things. It also eats away at stone, causing damage called **erosion**. Wind, frost and rain naturally cause erosion, but acid rain speeds it up. Many cities now have buildings and statues that are badly worn by acid rain.

The slightly acidic moisture is then deposited when it rains, hails or snows. Trees and plants soak up the tainted water through their roots. Rainwater also drains away into rivers and lakes, where it can kill fish and wildlife.

What can be done about acid rain? Lakes and forests are sometimes sprayed with lime, which counteracts the acid. But **'liming'** is expensive and only works for a time. The real solution is to reduce air pollution. In many countries, filters are now fitted to factory chimneys to remove pollutants. Since cars are part of the problem, everyone can help to reduce acid rain by using cars a bit less.

The details of this stone carving in London have been worn away by acid rain, so they are no longer clear.

How does pollution affect the soil?

The soil under our feet is a precious resource. Plants grow in the soil, providing food for animals and people. But soil can be polluted by waste from farming, industry and mining. It may also be **contaminated** by rubbish buried underground.

Most rubbish gets dumped in landfill sites like this one in Britain. When the site is full, it is covered with earth.

Mining can cause pollution. In a mining operation, huge amounts of soil and rock are removed to reach the valuable **minerals** below. Huge piles of waste rock build up around the mine. Chemicals used in the mining process can contaminate the land and also local rivers.

The huge amounts of rubbish we produce each week can cause pollution. Most rubbish gets buried in pits called **landfills**. These pits are meant to be leak-proof, but dangerous waste sometimes seeps into the soil. Countries such as Britain are also running out of places to put landfills.

DETECTIVE WORK

Do a rubbish survey at home. Separate your family's rubbish into food waste, paper and cardboard, glass, tins and plastic. Food waste such as fruit and vegetable peelings makes useful **compost**. Most other waste can now be recycled at a recycling centre.

Can you explain how insecticide could harm these birds?

Large hawks called goshawks prey on smaller birds that eat insects. These birds were harmed by DDT.

Love Canal

Between 1930 and 1950, an abandoned canal in eastern United States was used to dump dangerous chemicals. Then the canal was filled in, the land was sold, and houses were built there. By the mid-1970s people living in Love Canal had developed serious health problems. Poisonous chemicals were escaping from the ground. The site had to be abandoned.

Rubbish can be burned in furnaces called **incinerators**, but this can cause air pollution. We can help to tackle the problem of waste by trying to consume less and by **recycling** – see pages 26-27.

Chemicals used in farming may pollute the soil. Many farmers spray poisons called insecticides on their crops to kill plant-eating insects. The chemicals build up in the soil and are absorbed by plants and insects. Then they pass on up the food chain to affect larger animals. In the 1950s, a very powerful insecticide called DDT was sprayed onto crops. Later scientists discovered that DDT had passed up the food chain to weaken the eggs laid by hawks and eagles, so they could not breed successfully. DDT is now banned in most countries.

How does pollution affect rivers and seas?

Plants and animals need clean, fresh water. People also need water for drinking and washing. We also use water for farming, industry, transport and energy. However, human use of water leads to pollution.

Factories use river water for cleaning, cooling and manufacturing. Liquid waste from factories is sometimes poured directly into rivers. The current quickly carries the pollution downstream. However in many countries, it is now **illegal** to dump waste in rivers. Factories that use river water for cooling, for example for cooling hot metal, return warmer water to the river. The warm water can harm plants and animals. This is called **thermal** or heat pollution.

Check your local lake, pond or river for signs of pollution. Can you see any litter? Is the surface covered by weeds or scum? Frothy foam is caused by soap. A rainbow-coloured film is oil. Can you see healthy creatures, such as fish, dragonflies, frogs or birds along the banks?

Oil pollution

Oil is transported around the world by tanker. If a tanker is damaged in an accident, a major oil spill can occur. Such disasters make headline news. However, routine leaks from offshore oil rigs and oil tankers also cause considerable pollution.

This barrel on the beach contains toxic (poisonous) waste.

Chemicals used on farms, such as **pesticides** and fertilisers, drain off the land into streams and rivers. In some parts of the world, untreated **sewage** from towns also enters rivers. Both sewage and farm chemicals can cause tiny plants called **algae** to breed quickly. They smother the surface and use up oxygen in the water.

When rivers drain into the sea, the pollution ends up in coastal waters. The shallow seas close to land are the most polluted part of the oceans. Sewage and chemicals from the land make some beaches too dangerous for bathing. Rubbish, chemicals and even dangerous **radioactive** waste are sometimes dumped far out to sea. Currents and tides may spread the pollution far and wide.

How do you think the barrel in the picture opposite ended up on the beach?

Workers clean oil off a beach in South Wales following an oil spill in 1996. An oil tanker spilled the oil after hitting a rock.

What is global warming?

Scientists have recently discovered a change that is affecting environments everywhere. Temperatures all over the world are rising. This is called **global warming**. Almost all scientists are convinced that pollution is to blame.

Certain gases in the atmosphere trap the Sun's heat close to Earth's surface. This is called the **greenhouse effect**, and it helps to keep temperatures on Earth warm and comfortable. The gases that cause the effect are called **greenhouse gases**. Carbon dioxide is an important greenhouse gas.

The ice in glaciers like this one in Switzerland has started to melt because of global warming.

DETECTIVE WORK

Try this experiment to investigate the greenhouse effect. On a sunny day, leave a thermometer in the sun for ten minutes, then read the air temperature. Now place a large glass or clear plastic jar upside-down over the thermometer. Check the temperature again after ten minutes. The glass or plastic traps heat in a similar way to greenhouse gases in the atmosphere.

Low-lying islands such as the Maldives are threatened by rising sea levels.

Natural warming

Warming and cooling are a part of a natural cycle. Ever since the Earth formed, cold periods called **Ice Ages** have alternated with warmer periods. The last Ice Age peaked about 18,000 years ago. Since then, temperatures have risen slowly. However most scientists believe that temperatures are now rising faster than they would do naturally, because of pollution.

Now scientists have discovered we are adding more greenhouse gases to the atmosphere. As cars, power stations and factories burn fossil fuels, they give off carbon dioxide. This is increasing the natural greenhouse effect, and probably causing the warming.

Temperatures around the world rose by about 0.5°C in the last century. Temperatures have risen by more in the polar regions, and polar ice has started to melt as a result. The water in the oceans has also expanded as the seas have got warmer. All this is making sea levels rise. Sea levels rose by about 20 cm (8 inches) in the 20th century. If the pattern continues, low-lying coasts around the world could be at risk of flooding. Whole groups of islands, such as the Maldives in the Indian Ocean, could disappear beneath the waves.

Why is global warming a problem?

Experts cannot be sure about the effects of global warming. However many scientists believe the effects will be far-reaching. Weather patterns will probably be affected. Some plants and animals may lose their **habitats**. Farming will be affected too.

Some experts believe these golden toads died out because of global warming.

Scientists predict that temperatures will rise 2-4°C by the year 2100. An increase of 4°C would mean a significant rise in sea levels. Cities located on or near the coast, including London, New York, Venice (Italy) and Tokyo (Japan), could be at risk of flooding. Low-lying countries such as the Netherlands could lose a lot of land to the waves.

Effects on nature

Climate change is affecting plants and animals. The warm weather is making spring flowers like primroses bloom earlier. Birds are nesting sooner, and migrating birds such as swallows are arriving earlier. Some species are threatened with extinction because they cannot cope with climate change.

Forest fires such as this one in Los Angeles, United States often start during droughts. Some experts believe droughts are becoming more common because of global warming.

Meanwhile the weather seems to getting wilder and less predictable. This may also be because of global warming. Extreme storms such as hurricanes seem to be striking more often. Rainfall patterns are changing. Some places are being hit by floods because of extra-heavy rainfall. Other areas are experiencing bad droughts. Changeable weather patterns make it more difficult for farmers to grow crops.

So what can we do about global warming? Since the 1990s, world leaders have met several times to try to agree cuts in the amount of greenhouse gas each nation produces. However some nations refuse to agree to the cuts because they believe it will harm their industries. Part of the solution is to rely more on other forms of energy, such as solar energy, which don't produce greenhouse gases – see pages 24-25.

DETECTIVE WORK

Start to keep records of seasonal changes in your area. Note down the dates when spring flowers bloom. Record when migrating birds arrive in spring, and leave in autumn. Such records can help scientists work out the effects of climate change.

Are people the problem?

Pollution is a growing problem. Every year, there are more people on Earth, which inevitably leads to more pollution. Pollution also tends to increase as countries around the world develop their industries, and new factories and power stations open.

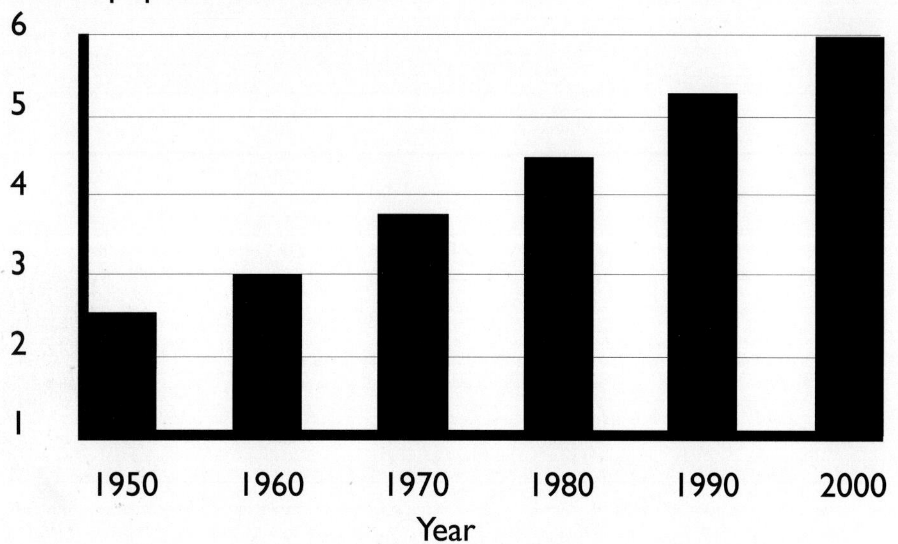

This graph shows the total world population from 1950 to 2000.

Study the graph. Did the population rise faster between 1950 and 1970 or between 1980 and 2000?

In 1999, Earth's **population** reached 6 billion. By 2013 it was 7.1 billion. As the population rises, so we need more houses and more food. Wild land is taken over to build towns and make more fields. Farmers also search for ways to make farming more efficient, so they can grow more food. This often means using more chemicals. The more people there are, the more resources are used to make all the things we need. This, too, causes pollution.

In more developed countries such as the United States and Britain, most families have at least one car. Homes contain all sorts of machines that make life easy and pleasant, such as fridges, washing machines, TVs and computers. Cars and other machines use energy and resources, which causes pollution. However, these countries can afford the technology that limits pollution.

DETECTIVE WORK

Find out about plans for new houses and developments in your area by logging on to the local council website. New developments may be built on wild land or on sites that have already been used. These are sometimes called 'brown field sites'.

Until recently, less developed countries such as India and China used less energy per person because people there had fewer cars and machines. But recently these nations have **industrialised** fast. People there also want the things that make life comfortable. However, there may be less money to spend on measures that limit pollution.

Wherever we live, we need to use resources and energy more carefully, and not waste them. Sharing anti-pollution technology can help to limit pollution.

Comparing energy use

In the United States every person currently uses as much energy as 13 Chinese people. The United States has just 4.5 per cent of the world's population. China has nearly 20 per cent. If everyone in China used as much energy as in the United States, it could lead to a massive amount of pollution.

This new estate on the outskirts of a city in the United States has been built on what was desert land.

What is being done to tackle pollution?

If people are causing pollution, it's up to all of us to find solutions! Before about 50 years ago, very few people thought about pollution. **Conservation** groups have helped to raise awareness of how pollution damages the air, water and soil. Now scientists, governments and many ordinary people are working to protect the environment.

These Greenpeace campaigners are telling people about climate change.

Since the 1960s and 1970s, many countries have passed laws to limit pollution. Pollution can be tackled in two different ways. Some measures aim to clean up pollution that is already happening. For example, dumping lime on a lake reduces the effects of acid rain. Other measures reduce pollution at the source. For example, factories fit filters to their chimneys to capture the pollution that leads to acid rain.

Lime is sprayed on to a lake in Sweden to counteract the effects of acid rain.

Burning fossil fuels for energy is a major cause of pollution. So are there other energy sources that cause less pollution? Nuclear energy is one alternative. But nuclear power plants produce waste that remains dangerous for thousands of years. Scientists haven't worked out how nuclear waste can be disposed of safely, so most of it is just buried underground.

Energy from the Sun, wind and flowing water can be used to generate electricity while causing much less pollution. Solar panels trap the Sun's energy to produce heat and electricity. Hydroelectric stations harness energy from fast-flowing rivers. Wind farms capture wind energy. These energy sources are called **'renewables'** because unlike coal, oil, gas and nuclear fuel, they will not run out.

DETECTIVE WORK

Greenpeace and Friends of the Earth are two conservation groups that are involved in fighting pollution. Find out more about their work by logging onto their websites.

International agreements

Some of the most important anti-pollution laws are international agreements, signed by many countries. In 1987, the Montreal Protocol helped to ban CFCs that were destroying ozone. In 1982, many European countries signed an agreement to reduce the pollution that causes acid rain. In 1997, the Kyoto Agreement set targets for many countries to limit their production of greenhouse gases.

How can I help to reduce pollution?

We all create some waste as we live our lives from day to day. Luckily, there are things that we can all do to limit pollution from waste, and the damage done to the air, water and soil. If everyone does just a little, it can add up to a huge amount.

Cycling can help to reduce pollution.

Most of the energy we use at home and at school comes from burning fossils fuels. We can all try to reduce air pollution by using energy more carefully. Try to switch off lights and machines such as computers when you're not using them. Using energy-saving lightbulbs is another way to reduce the amount of energy we use.

Vehicles cause a massive amount of pollution. Using cars less helps to limit the damage. Can you walk or cycle to school, or use public transport instead of a car? Or can you share car journeys with friends?

The waste water that leaves our homes is polluted by cleaning products such as bleach, soap powder and washing-up liquid. Everyone can reduce pollution by using cleaning products that are **'environmentally friendly'.**

Organic farming

Growing crops without using chemicals is called **organic farming**. Farmers use compost and manure to nourish crops instead of artificial fertiliser. Natural methods are used to control pests. Animals are reared on natural foods and usually allowed to roam freely. Discuss buying organic food with your family, or better still, try growing your own vegetables.

The rubbish we throw away is hard to get rid of, and can pollute the soil. Recycling glass, paper, plastic, cans and other materials reduces pollution. For example, when glass is recycled, old bottles and jars are smashed and reheated in a furnace to make new glass. This uses less energy, and also saves on the minerals used to make glass. This reduces pollution caused by mining.

Buying food that is produced locally saves on the pollution caused by transporting food.

DETECTIVE WORK

Eggs, meat, milk, grain, fruit and vegetables can all be grown organically. Textiles such as wool and cotton can also be produced in this way. See how many organic products you can find next time you go shopping.

Your project

If you've done the detective work and answered all of Sherlock's questions, you now know a lot about pollution! Investigate further by producing your own project about pollution.

First you'll need to choose a topic that interests you. You could take one of the following questions as a starting point.

Topic questions

- Find out all you can about one type of pollution. What is causing the problem? What are the effects?
- Compare the effects of one type of pollution in two different countries. One country could have many cities, the other could be a remote place, such as Antarctica. How do scientists measure pollution there? Is the problem being tackled in different ways?
- Investigate the effects of pollution at your school. Think about all the different types of pollution, including litter, and noise and light pollution. What could be done to tackle pollution at school? Would recycling help?
- Investigate different energy sources such as **hydroelectricity**. Which cause the least pollution? What are the advantages and disadvantages of each?

This hydroelectric dam on Loch Laggan in Scotland provides a renewable energy source.

Your local library and the Internet can provide all sorts of information to help you. Try the websites listed on page 31. When you have collected the information you need, present it in an interesting way. You might like to use one of the ideas below.

Project presentation

- People have different attitudes to pollution, especially when their work is involved. Write a short report about the topic from the point of view of one or two of the following: a factory owner, someone who works in a power station, a farmer, truck driver, scientist, wildlife expert or anti-pollution campaigner.
- Or you could write a poem or story about pollution from the point of view of an animal living in the affected environment.

Sherlock has found out about how his old enemy, the fox, is affected by litter. Some foxes live quite close to rubbish tips where they can find scraps of food. But best of all, like all animals, they like clean, unpolluted countryside.

This ranger at Johannesburg Lion Park in South Africa looks after white lion cubs.

Glossary

acid rain Rain that is slightly acidic because it is polluted by waste gases in the atmosphere.
algae Tiny plants, many types of which grow in water.
atmosphere A layer of gases that surrounds the Earth.
catalytic converter Device which reduces waste gases when fitted to vehicle exhausts.
CFCs Short for chlorofluorocarbons, a group of chemicals that attack ozone.
compost Natural materials which rot to make fertiliser for plants.
conservation Work done to protect the natural world.
contaminated Polluted.
dispose To get rid of something like litter.
environment The surroundings in which we live.
environmentally friendly Of a substance that does not harm the natural world.
erosion The wearing away of rock, earth or stone surfaces by water, wind, ice or pollution.
fossil fuel A fuel such as coal, oil, and natural gas, which are made of fossilised plants or animals that lived millions of years ago.
global warming Rising temperatures worldwide, caused by an increase of gases in the atmosphere that trap the Sun's heat.
greenhouse effect The warming effect caused by certain gases in the atmosphere, which prevent the Sun's heat, reflected by the Earth, from escaping into space.
greenhouse gases Gases in the atmosphere that trap the Sun's heat. Carbon dioxide is an important greenhouse gas.
habitat A particular place where plants and animals live, such as a rainforest or desert.
hydroelectricity When electricity is made using energy from flowing water.
illegal Of an action that is against the law.
Ice Age A long period when the climate was cooler than it is now.
incinerator A hot furnace in which rubbish is burned.
industrialise When a country develops its industries, so that many factories and power plants open.
landfill A pit in the ground where rubbish is buried.
liming When lime is dropped on a lake or forest to neutralise the effects of acid rain.
manufacture To make something, usually in a factory.
minerals Non-living natural substances.
organic farming A method of farming without using chemicals.
ozone layer A layer of ozone gas found in the atmosphere, which prevents harmful ultraviolet rays in sunlight from reaching Earth.
population The number of people living in a certain place.
pesticides Chemicals put on plants to kill plant-eating pests.
pollutant Substance that harms the air, water, or land.
pollution Any harmful substance that damages the environment.
radioactive Of a material that gives off dangerous radiation.
raw materials Natural materials such as minerals or timber, that are processed in factories.
recycling When rubbish is saved and remade into a new product.
renewables Natural energy sources that will not get used up.
sewage Dirty water from homes, containing chemicals and human waste.
smog A poisonous, dirty haze that forms in the air when polluting gases react with sunlight.
thermal To do with heat.
toxic Poisonous.
ultraviolet rays Harmful rays in sunlight which can cause health problems for animals and people.
water vapour Moisture in the form of a gas.

Answers

Page 6: The brightly-lit areas are cities. The darker areas on land have fewer cities and towns.

Page 9: Seals prey on fish, and are eaten by polar bears.

Page 15: Insecticide is absorbed by plants. Plant-eating insects absorb the poison, which then passes to birds that eat the insects. The poison builds up in hawks that eat many contaminated birds.

Page 17: The barrel was probably dumped far out to sea. Waves, tides and currents have carried it to shore and washed it up on the beach.

Page 22: The world population went up by 1.2 billion between 1950 and 1970. It rose by 1.6 billion between 1980 and 2000 – faster than during the earlier period.

Further Information

Further reading

Protecting Our Planet: Energy in Crises by Catherine Chambers (Wayland, 2009)

Protecting Our Planet: Toxins in the Food Chain by Sarah Levete (Wayland, 2009)

Understanding Pollution: Oil Spills by Lucy Poddington (Franklin Watts, 2006)

Understanding Pollution: Acid Rain by Lucy Poddington (Franklin Watts, 2006)

Your Environment: Pollution by Cindy Leaney (Franklin Watts, 2005)

Websites

US Environment Protection Agency
www.epa.gov/kids/
UK Environment Agency
www.environment-agency.gov.uk/

Environment Protection Authority, Australia
www.environment.gov.au

The Young People's Trust for the Environment
A charity which aims to encourage young people's understanding of the environment and the need for sustainability.
www.ypte.org.uk/

Environmental fact sheet from The Young People's Trust for the Environment
www.ypte.org.uk/environmental/environment-how-can-you-help-protect-it-/81
Information on acid rain:
www.ypte.org.uk/environmental/acid-rain/1

The Soil Association
An organisation involved in organic farming.
www.soilassociation.org

Conservation groups involved in fighting pollution and protecting wildlife

Greenpeace UK
www.greenpeace.org.uk

Friends of the Earth
www.foe.co.uk

Worldwide Fund for Nature
www.wwf.org.uk/

Index

The numbers in **bold** refer to pictures